RENZO CHIARELLI

D0993500

ASSISI

AND THE BASILICA OF
SAN FRANCESCO

Translated by
PAUL GARVIN

BONECHI EDITORE

50122 FIRENZE - Via dei Rustici, 5

ASSISI

Seen from afar from the other side of the valley — from the hills around Perugia or from Perugia itself — Assisi seems to be a large greyish blot on the slope of Mount Subasio (which reminds you of a huge sprawling whale with its curved back), like a stone quarry of unusual size. Then as you gradually approach, the blot or the quarry expands and acquires shape and proportion; it divides into hundreds of crevices, cliffs, gulfs, defiles, chasms and ramifications, until you begin to realise that they are really houses, towers, streets, belfries and gardens. Then all at once when you see them clearly, you are filled with wonder and astonishment at the miracle of an ancient town that is still alive in our day, famous and venerated the world over. The one thing that does not change with nearness is the colour, the peculiar colour of Assisi, a mixture of pink and grey like chalk and mother-of-pearl, the same lovely hues that can be seen in the incrustations on the fragile sides of ancient amphorae recovered after long years buried in the sea. It is the pink, the white, the grey and the violet of the stone and marble of Subasio which makes the extaordinary blend into a single variegated whole under the sun and rarified air of summer and the frosts and winds of winter.

What can one say about Assisi after all this time, a place so justly famous and so often praised, without repeating clichés? Only that here St. Francis was born, without enlarging upon the enormous spiritual and historical consequences of the fact, and that Francis gave birth to Giotto and the Basilica, and with them to Italian art. In Assisi two things are united; a mystical experience of the highest order, probably the greatest after that of Christ, and a glorious civic history throughout the ages — from early times under the Umbrians and Etruscans, the birthplace of Sextus Propertius under the Romans, then a free commune continually at war with its neigbour Perugia, a Ghibelline stronghold loyal to Barbarossa and his son Frederick, disputed between feudal lords and mercenary captains until for long centuries it was part of the papal dominions. But Assisi became great and eternal from the moment it gave birth to the « sun » *whose wondrous life were better sung in the glory of heaven.* From then on Francis was Assisi and Assi-

si Francis. His name made Assisi a city of the spirit, a church open to the world.

It is an extraordinary town, where the streets climb up and down contrarywise and, just like the houses, seem to be carved by main force out of the hillside, and the houses of stone and brick lie huddled up together with an almost forbidding appearance redeemed by the festive profusion of roses and geraniums flowering everywhere on walls and windowsills and balconies. It is a town overflowing with convents and churches that are among the most splendid of the Italian Middle Ages and drew here Cimabue and Giotto, the Roman pupils of Pietro Cavallini, and the Sienese Pietro Lorenzini and Simone Martini to offer their labours in homage to Francis and Clare.

All around Assisi on hill and plain the powerful air of « green Umbria » can be sensed. The last war left it miraculously intact when the invading armies passed within sight of it, and even more miraculously the great sea of concrete that is spreading irresistibly all over the rest of Italy has halted before it as if ashamed to raise its impudent head.

Assisi, « God's citadel » and the new Jerusalem, where art, nature and faith are wedded in Franciscan serenity. **Pax et bonum:** where you can breathe an unaccustomed air for our day, and all belongs to this extraordinary atmosphere, not only the sublime things and the Franciscan memories but also the small humble things, like the swallows nestling at San Damiano, the turtle doves at the Porziuncola, the few square yards of Clare's garden, her veiled nuns who from behind the grating in the church make large mysterious signs with their arms for you to approach. A town in which you can go indifferently to pray to St. Francis or to see Giotto, but in which (as has been said before) you run the risk of wanting to become a saint in earnest.

3

THE BASILICA OF SAN FRANCESCO

All the streets in Assisi seem to lead to the Basilica, whether they reach it quickly from the main square or wind their way among silent flower-covered houses or flow down from the hilltop of the fortress and Porta San Giacomo or ascend from below, skirting the walls and passing through the triumphal gates, as if converging into a huge comb or seeking a reason for their existence in the great green open space anciently known as *collis inferni* (the mouth of Hell). Here in the Basilica is the spiritual heart of Assisi and

of Italy. Here art was born in Italy in the name of the saintly son of Pietro di Bernardone. The tall soaring façade gleams in the sun with the brightness of the marble, illuminated by the delicate subtle interlacing of the perforated arabesques in the gleaming rose-window in the centre, and guarded on one side by the massive square-shaped tower (once adorned with a pointed top), while the magnificent Gothic-arched double doorway rounded by trilobed arches opens to welcome the unceasing flow of pilgrims that have been

coming here for centuries. It is a pilgrimage which has continued from generation to generation since the body of St. Francis was solemnly laid in the lower church, begun hardly two years previously, on May 25th, 1230.

CONSTRUCTION

According to tradition the architect of the Basilica — or rather of the two superimposed basilicas — was Frate Elia of Assisi, who was General of the Franciscan Order from 1232 to 1239 and received a donation of a piece of land from Simone di Pucciarello in 1228 for the construction of the church and convent. Modern historians and critics, however, take the view that the actual architect was someone else (Filippo di Campello according to some), a man who being experienced in French Gothic introduced something of its external design and rhythm, but who above all had in mind the great tradition of Italian Romanesque which is so evident in the interior spacing. It was from the amalgamation of opposing ideas that the Basilica became the birthplace of Italian Gothic architecture. It may be that Frate Elia inspired and supervised the memorable undertaking, and he was urged on and encouraged by Pope Gregory IX who on 12th July 1228, shortly after Francis's canonization, laid the foundation stone of the building.

The two basilicas are joined by a double flight of steps on the side of the tower. Behind the apse and around the 15th century cloister stands the massive square block of the convent, solemnly planted on the rock on a long stretch of pylons and arches. It was constructed in the second half of the 14th century, probably by Matteo Gattapone da Gubbio, and never ceases to fill the visitor with wonder on his first arrival in Assisi.

THE LOWER CHURCH

There is still some doubt about the dates when the two churches were built. The lower one must have already been in a condition to house the saint's body in 1230, and the whole structure was presumably covered over by 1235, the year that the church was consecrated by Gregory IX (in 1236 Frate Elia had a crucifix painted by Giunta Pisano which unfortunately disappeared in the 18th century). At any rate it may be considered that the main architectural structure of the whole basilica was more or less complete when Innocent IV solemnly dedicated it on May 25th, 1253. The lower church is naturally the one which is more Romanesque in character. Its function, well expressed by the imposing structure, the calculated distribution of light, and the lowness of the vaulting, is to produce an amosphere of awe and mystery. This is enhanced by the complexity of the groundplan as a result of the chapels added later towards the end of the 13th century, and by the lengthening of the sides in the area of the counter-façade.

The great pointed-arched double door of the Basilica of San Francesco, and the magnificent round window in the centre of the façade (on the sides, the symbols of the evangelists. This beautiful « eye » of the church, with its fine decoration of concentric rings of marble resembling a Gothic ivory, is the first point to which the visitor's attention is instinctively drawn, and it is this type of rose-window, to be found in so many other churches of Assisi, that forms the *leit-motiv* of architecture in the town.

THE UPPER CHURCH

Entering the upper church is always a source of joy, surprise and consolation at the sight that is presented: the ample measured space felicitously confined within a single nave, the perfect measuring of the vaults and wing-spans to which the upward dividing of the tall pillars adds a fullness of rhythm, a calm and solemnity altogether human. (It is not difficult to recognise the French, or to be more precise, Angevin models in the formation of the capitals as in the circular and semi-circular towers outside). But joy and wonder come above all from the light which proudly enters from the great windows, filtering through the stained glass and spreading through and through, and from the magic of the colour, soft, vibrant and kaleidoscopical, that the light generates as it covers every inch of the walls and vaults in the nave, sanctuary and apse, revealing the most astonishing, perhaps the greatest and most complete story in painting that the human mind has ever conceived. An unreal and resplendent atmosphere is produced by the malachite coloured patches on the starry blue of the vaults, as of a marine background.

The architectural pattern of the upper church is in the form of a Latin cross with a single nave, with fluted columns supporting the ogival vaults stretching up to the polygonal nave.
On the walls at either side are 28 stories of St. Francis frescoed by Giotto and his assistants. The most important of these are shown in the following pages.

THE CYCLE OF PAINTINGS

The Cross commissioned by Frate Elia from Giunta Pisano in 1236 (removed in 1623 and finally lost in the following century) was almost certainly the first painting made for the Basilica of San Francesco, and hence the first step that the church itself was to take in becoming the greatest monument of Italian painting. Giunta Pisano was the forerunner of the unknown painter who in the second half of the century, probably after 1220, frescoed the walls of the lower church with the lively **Stories of St. Francis** and **Scenes of the Passion** (unfortunately damaged by the opening up of the side chapels). He is the so-called **Maestro di San Francesco**, a sensitive Umbrian artist to whom we therefore owe the first great cycle of paintings dedicated to Francis, which Giotto must have been aware of when he set about his **Franciscan Stories** in the upper church.

The real painting of the church began, however, under the Orsini pope, Nicholas III, and especially under Nicholas IV (the first Franciscan pope) when the decoration of the upper church was undertaken. Cimabue arrived from Florence with his pupils (c. 1278, or even a decade later according to others) for the grand task of decorating the apse and transept (**Stories of Mary, Stories from the Apocalypse, Acts of SS. Peter and Paul**); the great **Crucifixion** in the left transept and the other, with considerable help, in the right one; also the **Evangelists** on the sanctuary vault with **Angelic Theories** etc.). In the lower church the large fresco of the **Madonna Enthroned, Angels and Saints** is his as well. The presence in Assisi of Cimabue, the first great innovator of Florentine painting, was a determining factor, but he was soon followed by teams of artists from Rome from the flourishing school directed by Pietro Cavallini (among them may have been Filippo Rusati and Jacopo Torriti). Assisi thus became the melting-pot in which the two main currents of art in Italy at the time were fused — though the presence also of Duccio di Buoninsegna, the leading figure of the Sienese school cannot be altogether excluded — and their encounter meant that the Basilica of San Francesco became the starting-point for the complete renewal of painting that was shortly to take place. It is generally agreed that, besides the **tondi** in the vault of the second span, the work of the Roman artists is chiefly to be found in the first panels with **Stories from the Old Testament** (legible beginning from the transept) on the upper part of the right wall, and in some of the **Stories from the New Testament** on the wall opposite (e.g. the **Wedding at Cana**); while the other scenes in the upper right and left sections can mostly be taken as Cimabue's contribution, though here again they have been attributed to a host of others. For the two magnificent **Stories of Isaac**, for example, a highly controversial figure with the conventional name of **Maestro d'Isaaco** has been invented. The very high quality of some of these scenes — among them the **Stories of Joseph**, the **Stories of Isaac** just mentioned and, on the left wall, the dramatic **Mourning over the Body of Christ**, and others — and the striking novelty of the language in which they are expressed have led many critics to attribute them to Giotto — a youthful Giotto who was present in Assisi in Cimabue's company during the years 1290-93.

« MAESTRO DI SAN FRANCESCO »: **Preaching to the Birds** (*lower church*). ▶

The mystical poetry of the « Little Flowers » seems to be transposed into this moving scene (one of the most striking miracles in the saint's life) which was painted with a lightness of touch and a liveliness of inspiration by the « Maestro di San Francesco » in the 60's of the 13th century. Giotto was inspired to a certain extent by this fresco for his painting on the same subject in the upper church.

CIMABUE: **Crucifixion** (*upper church*).

Like the greater part of Cimabue's frescoes in the transept in the upper church, this powerful and dramatic **Crucifixion** has suffered irreparable damage with the passing of time, chiefly owing to the oxidization of the white lead. The bright colours have become blackened so as to give the painting the startling appearance of a photographic negative. In spite of this the work is one of the highlights of late 13th century Italian painting and one of Cimabue's greatest masterpieces.

GIOTTO: **Isaac rejecting Esau** (*upper church*). ▶

The two **Stories of Isaac** on the upper part of the right wall, for which Coletti had proposed the conventional figure of a so-called « Maestro d'Isacco », have now been attributed to Giotto in his youth (c. 1290) by a large number of modern critics. The two episodes share with the other bible scenes in this row in creating a biblical atmosphere rich in poetic content with a moral and human sense of assuredness that is something new, and a calm and solemn majesty. This and the sharp precision of spatial design has moved critics, though with some reserve, to recognise the presence of a hand that can hardly be that of anyone else but Giotto.

GIOTTO IN THE UPPER CHURCH

Unfortunately some of these famous frescoes have disappeared and the majority are in such a poor condition as to make it extremely difficult to examine them properly. It is this that makes adequate criticism of them a highly debatable matter and still leaves the authorship of them an open question.

At any rate we know Giotto was at Assisi in 1296. According to Vasari he was summoned there by the Franciscan General, Fra Giovanni da Muro. He too was now in the stage of « renewal » after his experience in Rome and the influence of Cavallini, and especially of Arnolfo. Between 1296 and 1298-1300 he produced the twenty-eight marvellous **Franciscan Stories** along the lower part of the walls in the upper church from the transept to the front and back again

to the transept. Vasari credited Giotto with the whole of the thirty-two scenes, but four of them — the first from the transept on the right wall and the last three on the left towards the transept. — are attributed by critics today to one of his associates, the so-called **Maestro della Santa Cecilia.** The problem of collaboration in these Franciscan Stories is a much debated one and still far from being solved. The presence of pupils is quite evident in many cases, but it is just as evident that the unifying idea of the cycle, the revolutionary method of composition, the daring use of space perspective, the original attempts at monumental plasticism, the human and spiritual intensity of the figures, and finally the design itself of all the scenes, all point to a single mind — Giotto's — directing and co-ordinating the

whole. To him must also be ascribed the clear slender architectural designs (small twisted columns, brackets, ceiling-work, etc.) which with the evident intention of creating illusionary perspective, often with the aid of « Cosmati » motifs, serve as frames for each of the « stories », under which by way of explanation there were once inscriptions in Latin (these have now quite disappeared but survive in the reconstruction made by Padre Mariangeli). The narration is based on the model of St. Bonaventure's **Legenda Maior** (c. 1260). It departs· from the ascetic spirit of the « Little Flowers » and strikes a heroic and strongly humanised note in its portrayal of the life of Francis. The artist only partly follows the suggestions of previous Franciscan iconography, though he does not ignore those that may have come to him from the « stories » in the lower church by the **Maestro di San Francesco.**

Is Giotto the painter of the « Franciscan Stories »? There was never any doubt about the matter, tradition and historical evidence were unanimous on the point. That Giotto was responsible for them was never questioned, at least until the 19th century when critics like Witte and Rumhor began to express the first doubts and were followed by others who advanced increasingly convincing theories to the contrary. Though the majority of critics today still uphold the claim for Giotto, there are not a few (such as Rintelen and Offner) who maintain a negative position. It may be said that, though in many scenes there is evidence of a great deal of help from others which at times even appears to be paramount, it is difficult to imagine any painter so advanced at the time other than Giotto who, to quote Salvini, in these " Franciscan Stories " « aims at creating a plastic synthesis to contain all phenomenal appearance and the physical quality itself of nature and man of which he was intensely aware, halting each time the continuity of the story in a firm architecture of masses with the enthusiasm of a new discovery and a candid wonder at the miracle of reality... it is this that assures the Giotto of Assisi a rightful place among the ' primitives ' » (turn to page 30).

◀ Another striking episode in the history of this unique monument of art was the completion of the magnificent stained-glass windows, both in the upper church (the earliest ones, by French and Italian craftsmen from the middle to the end of the 13th century) and in the lower, these the work of artists from central Italy in the first half of the 14th century. Simone Martini himself supplied the cartoons for the windows in the St. Martin Chapel, the whole of which he frescoed.

Upper Basilica of San Francesco. The vault sails of the fourth span, decorated by finely-wrought coloured bands, show the four Doctors of the Church exercising their ministry before a corresponding number of clerics. These frescoes were once thought to be by Rusuti but are now attributed to co-workers of Giotto in his early manner.

MAESTRO DELLA SANTA CECILIA: **Francis receiving the homage of the simple man** (*upper church*).

This scene (the first in the lower row starting from the transept) opens the series of the life of Francis, though it was painted at a later date by the « Maestro della Santa Cecilia », a follower and fellow-worker of Giotto, probably after the latter's departure from Assisi, but undoubtedly from a design made by him. The background is an imaginary Assisi, recognizable from the presence of two of the most characteristic buildings in the town - the Temple of Minerva and the tower of the 'Capitano del Popolo'. The saint (already such in the eyes of God and therefore distinguished by a golden halo) walks with dignity and assurance and, unlike the bystanders, appears to be unsurprised at the homage paid to him by « the simple man » (*homo simplex* in the Latin inscription) who is spreading his cloak before his feet, as if divinely inspired to recognize the youth's predestined sanctity.

GIOTTO: **The Gift of the Cloak** (*upper church*).

This celebrated episode also takes place in the open, without witnesses, in a calm and peaceful natural setting. Francis meets an impoverished gentleman and, moved with sudden pity, makes him a gift of his cloak. Alighting from his horse, the saint is preparing to make the compassionate gesture. The other bows with surprise and deference. The cloak, drawn in space by a flowing of thick folds, is descending between the two of them, while the horse, arching its neck with a most natural gesture, is bending down in search of a clump of grass. Never before have nature and landscape seemed to share so directly in a human action: the two rough stony hills converging diagonally at the centre, the chapel with the pointed spire, and the astonishing picture of a walled town (Assisi) whose compact forms already mark the triumph of solid geometry.

GIOTTO: **St. Francis and the Crucifix in San Damiano** (*upper church*).

« *As Francis was praying before an image of the Crucified One, a voice came down from the Cross and said three times: " Francis, go and repair my house which is all falling into ruin," meaning by this the Roman Church* ».

Francis is kneeling before the Byzantine crucifix in San Damiano; the church is all in ruins, the walls open, the roof uncovered; against it towers the magnificent figure of the saint, purposely filling all the space with light. It is to him alone that the miraculous crucifix is speaking, asking him to restore his Church. Already in this scene we can recognize the consolidation of Giotto's awareness of space which has rightly been pointed out as « one of the chief features of his work taken as a whole » (D. Gioseffi).

GIOTTO: **Renouncement of Worldly Goods** (*upper church*).

...« when he gave back everything to his father and, stripping himself, renounced his father's and the world's goods ».

The centralness of the episode, so well indicated by the empty space into which converge the retreating lines of the buildings that serve as stage-wings to the scene, depends as much on the perspective as on its moral and historical implications when we realise that Francis's definite and total separation from worldly ties and attachments was the crucial point at which his life as a saint really begins. The crowd is hedged around him, startled and puzzled; Pietro di Bernardone, hardly to be restrained, is rushing angrily at his son, but Francis seems already projected towards a higher dimension, his face inspired and his arms upraised, as if quite unaware of his nakedness which the embarassed Bishop of Assisi is trying his best to cover. In the studied, well-modelled figure of the nude Francis and the thickset, threatening figure of his father there is already the announcement of Giotto's re-appreciation of the human figure in a corporeal as well as a moral sense. .

GIOTTO: **Approval of the Franciscan Rule** (*upper church*).

There is in this fresco a direct confirmation of Giotto's " spatiality " in the sense of a studied rational perception of geometrical perspective and a restitution of space by means of the perspective (examples can be noted in the masterly construction of the arches in the upper part and the foreshortening of the corbels). The importance of the occasion is made evident by the deep concentration shown by the pope (Innocent III) surrounded by bishops and cardinals in full regalia in contrast to the humble poorly-clad group of Franciscans, upon whom the pope's eloquent and solemn gesture of assent descends by way of Francis, whose ardent figure is the real focal point of the composition.

GIOTTO: **Driving out of the devils from Arezzo** (*upper church*).

The main character in the scene is really the town from which the horrifying devils are fleeing as if sucked up from on high. There is no doubt about its being Arezzo, with the houses and towers climbing the steep ascent up to the Pretorian Palace. In the peremptory way the large volumetrical masses confront each other (the town and the church on the left) the human figures seem to increase in significance. Originating from Francis and working through the powerful gigantic figure of the exorcist, the miracle takes place along a diagonal line running upwards from the bottom with a suggestion of space that is more mental than real.

GIOTTO: **The Crib at Greccio** (*upper church*).

The episode of the crib (the first of its kind) that Francis made at Greccio in memory of the birth of Jesus is a central point in his life for its poetic nature and the still unbroken traditional custom it gave rise to. Though we can find evidence of collaboration in this scene, the artist's poetic feeling and imagination combine to produce an emotion of tenderness new in painting and touched with a lyrical freshness hitherto unknown. The artist appears induced by the exceptionalness of the subject to relate the story with loving devotion and extraordinary delicacy. Apart from the rapid tempo of the composition and the inimitable series of exercises in perspective (the ambo, the tabernacle, the foreshortened picture of the cross), the fundamental interest of the scene is concentrated in the mute colloquy between the saint and the miraculous babe, producing a timeless ineffable atmosphere in which the human and the divine fade into each other.

GIOTTO: **The Miracle of the Thirsty Man** (*upper church*).

The dominant theme of the religious symbolism in the whole of the Franciscan cycle is the role of intermediary between heaven and earth, and is represented in this scene of the **Miracle of the Thirsty Man** in which Francis is once more the geometric centre of the composition as well as the moral pivot of the episode in the way he is anxiously leaning forward, in the certainty of being heard, to invoke the miracle of the restoring water which will gush forth from the rock. In contrast to the static and puzzled-looking figures of the two stout friars on the left there is that of the thirsty man, leaping forward and describing an arc in space, ready to throw himself wildly on the spring. The action takes place in a barren abstract landscape designed to convey the nightmarish quality of the scene.

GIOTTO: **Preaching to the Birds** (*upper church*).

« *And he went into the field and began to preach to the birds that were on the ground, and at once those that were on the trees came down to him, and they all stood still together until St. Francis finished preaching, and then they would not go away until he gave them his blessing* » (from the « Little Flowers »).

This most famous of the stories of Francis is a calm and peaceful one, with the saint isolated in a great silent space in subdued conversation with nature and his beloved creatures, the chattering birds flitting down and hopping about on the ground, curious and attentive with heads upturned - real birds drawn from life, unlike the birds in Byzantine ikons looking like rows of notes on a musical scale.

◀ GIOTTO: **Death of the Lord of Celano** (*upper church*).

The sudden end of the Lord of Celano, struck dead during supper after he had made his confession and been assured by Francis of eternal salvation, shows the tragical climax of the Franciscan cycle and is therefore the most dramatic of Giotto's scenes before those of the Passion at Padua. It is full of throbbing anguish and desperation, and foreshadows much of what was to come in religious painting in the two heads of the lord and his wife drawn close together, and the figure with clasped hands and loosened hair which seems to anticipate the Magdalen at Padua, and the choral explosion of the stony-faced crowd to which Francis, standing upright, forms a wonderful counterpoise in the enclosure of a perfectly-formed intangible space.

In the harmonious setting of the Renaissance Cloister, probably built by Antonio da Como between 1472 and 1474 on the orders of Sixtus IV, the great apse of the Basilica stands in solemn grandeur with its elegant Gothic windows and flanked by stout round towers.

29

The sacristy of the lower Basilica, on the vault of which an unknown follower of Giotto (the « Maestro delle Vele ») frescoed the allegories of the Franciscan *Virtues*. In the left transept are the frescoes of Pietro Lorenzetti, and the seventeenth-century ones of Sermei on the vault of the apse.

A crypt was dug under the lower church in 1822-24 to allow access to **the saint's tomb** which had been discovered in 1818 (its present arrangement dates from 1925). Around that of Francis, the tombs of his faithful companions — Fra Leone, Fra Ruffino, Fra Masseo and Frate Angelo — have now been laid.

GIOTTESQUE AND SIENESE PAINTERS IN THE LOWER CHURCH

At the turn of the century Giotto left Assisi for Rome in view of the Jubilee proclaimed by Boniface VIII in 1300 (the one recorded by Dante in the Inferno). His pupils remained behind, chief among them the **Maestro della Santa Cecilia**, but it is almost certain that he made a return visit round about 1313 during the de-

coration of the **Magdalen Chapel** which had just been constructed by Cardinal Partino da Montefiore. Some parts of the decoration are of such high quality as to leave little doubt about his direct participation in them. The rapid construction of chapels along the walls and at the transept ends had transformed the lower church into an extraordinary kind of art factory on full scale production in which the whole of Giotto's Florentine workshop was employed. One of his unknown workers (the **Maestro delle Vele**) did the splendid **Franciscan Allegories** in the cross-vault above the altar; the **Maestro di Figline** decorated one of the sacristies with a **Madonna and Saints**; Stefano, the foremost of Giotto's pupils, and also author of the **Crucifixion** in the convent chapter house, began work on a **Glory of Paradise** in the apse which was to be destroyed in 1628, and probably on the underarch of the pulpit. It was the same **Maestro delle Vele** who frescoed the **Stories of Christ's Childhood** in the right arm of the transept, while others of Giotto's school decorated the San Ni-

colò Chapel. But Florentines were not the only ones working in the lower church. The arrival of the Sienese had its share in making it the magnificent collection of Central Italian paintings of the Trecento. While between 1321 and c. 1329 the Sienese Pietro Lorenzetti executed the delightful mural tryptych in the Orsini Chapel and undertook the decoration of its walls and vault (the dramatic **Scenes of the Passion, Figures of Saints,** etc.), Simone Martini did a masterly painting of the memorable episode of the beggar in the life of St. Martin in the chapel dedicated to that saint (1322-26). He was also responsible for the mystical portrait of **St. Catherine** and the three other half-figures of saints in the transept of the lower church. The last

14th century painter to work in the lower church was Andrea da Bologna who with a pupil frescoed the St. Catherine of Alessandria Chapel.

CIMABUE: **St. Francis** (*Detail of the fresco in the lower church*).

« St. Francis is a masterpiece of the art of portrayal even though he is depicted in a fanciful manner by the artist who was too young to have known him as he really was. What matters is that he is a well-construct- ed person visually adequate to his mission. There is a world of difference from the interpretations of the Byzantine type which had stylized him into a primordial, esoteric figure... In the Franciscan Order as well, at least in Assisi, the most serious crisis had now been overcome, the trumpets of the Apocalypse had ceased their blast, and the monastic organization was more than ever developing its social action. And the saint in Cimabue's fresco walks on the hard earth, barefoot, with pierced hands, clasping the book of truth, small in size, without displaying it as a transcendent attribute » (E. Battisti, *Cimabue*, 1963).

PIETRO LORENZETTI: **Crucifixion** (*lower church*).

The most dramatic period of Pietro Lorenzetti's art is to be found in the great cycle with his **Stories of the Passion** in the left arm of the transept in the lower church, which he was able to infuse with such an ardent sense of pathos as to make them « one of the highest witnesses to the dramatic genius of the Italian Trecento » (E. Carli). The scenes most densely packed with emotion and pathos are undoubtedly those of the **Crucifixion** and the **Deposition.** In his « Lives » the great 16th century historian Vasari gives this pithy description of the **Crucifixion** (which however he wrongly attributed to Pietro Cavallini): « *A Crucifixion of Jesus Christ with armed horsemen in various styles and with a great variety of extravagant dress, and of divers foreign countries. In the air he made some angels who are weeping bitterly as they rest on their wings in different attitudes; and some clasping their hands to their breasts, others joining them together, and others beating the palms against each other, demonstrate their utmost grief at the death of the Son of God; and all from the middle backwards or from the middle downwards are converted into air* ».

PIETRO LORENZETTI: **Madonna with Child between SS. Francis and John the Evangelist** (*lower church*).

The charming tryptych of Pietro Lorenzetti that serves to adorn the great frescoes in the left arm of the transept in the lower church (c. 1326-29) is one of the most justly famous of this delicate yet vigorous artist who here once again displays his extraordinary ability in blending a refined musicality of line peculiar to Siena with a suggestion of robustness to be found in Giotto and Florentine painting. The splendid paleness of the colouring, the dextrous rhythm of the composition, the mute affectionate colloquy between the persons, their affable gestures (the Virgin pointing out Francis's stigmata to the Child), the detached poetic nature of the scene, all make this painting one of the most significant expressions of Italian 14th century art.

SIMONE MARTINI (*lower church*): ▶
page 36 - **St. Martin made a Knight**
page 37 - **St. Martin leaving the Army**

In the frescoes covering all the wall space in the St. Martin Chapel Simone Martini, the greatest Sienese painter of the 14th century, admirably illustrated the life of the soldier saint, anticipating with assurance the themes and motifs of Gothic chivalry and courtliness. The charm of the colouring and the subtle modulation of line are here united to a profound awareness of plastic and spiritual values, and the artist's imagination soars to unusual heights. « The episodes most delicately changing colour recur in the group of musicians and the long coat of the capped flute player, in the emperor with his medal-like profile and blue cloak, and in the soldier with the striped cap and green jacket which stands out so elegantly against the saint's violet tunic » (E. Cecchi, *Trecentisti Senesi*).

SIMONE MARTINI: **St. Clare** (*lower church*).

This « ideal portrait » of the spiritual companion of St. Francis was painted by Simone Martini together with four other pictures of saints (Francis, Ludwig of Toulouse, Elizabeth of Hungary and Louis of France) probably after he had finished the great work in the St. Martin Chapel. It is one of the most delicately poetic and spiritual of paintings that Gothic art has left us. « In his taste for the common people », as the critic Emilio Cecchi noted, « it may be said that some of his saints, especially St. Francis and St. Clare, together with the Angel in the **Annunciation** in the Uffizi, are a summary of the whole repertory and of the glory of Simone Martini ».

« MAESTRO DELLE VELE »: **Espousal with Poverty** (*lower church*).

In the « sails » of the cross-vault in the lower church, above the high altar, an unknown collaborator of Giotto, particularly inclined towards ostentatious decoration with gold backgrounds and so forth, painted four « allegories » in fresco intended to glorify St. Francis and the basic virtues of the Franciscan Order (**Espousal with Poverty, Allegories of Chastity and Obedience, Apotheosis of the Saint**). These « allegories » have long been the subject of animated discussion by critics - in the past they were attributed to Giotto himself - and today they are considered to be by one of his followers, a painter who shows a certain amount of Sienese influence, the so-called « Maestro delle Vele », and who is also evident in some of the frescoed scenes in the left transept vault. The most illuminating, and perhaps the most celebrated, of the « allegories » is the one depicting the **Saint's Espousal with Poverty**, an extraordinarily imaginative painting packed with abstract medieval Christian symbolism.

VISITING THE CITY

PIAZZA DEL COMUNE (*Town Hall Square*). The square is similar in character to that of other squares in the Umbrian and Tuscan towns of central Italy. It is in the shape of an irregular rectangle on a ridge of the hill and on a line with the only street which can be called almost level (or at least less steep than the others) and which recalls the « **Rugapiana** » of the not far distant Cortona. At the upper end where two of the largest streets join stands a fine spraying fountain; on the lower side — the more « fashionable » part with its cafés and shops — the **Palazzo dei Priori** extends in four separate blocks with its adornment of coats-of-arms and emblematic designs, and the noble-looking battlements restored in recent times. It houses the **Pinacoteca Civica** (Civic Picture Gallery) which deserves to be better known and appreciated for the valuable collection it holds. The keynote of the square, however, is to be found on the side opposite where stands the 13th century **Palazzo del Capitano del Popolo** with the beauty of its slim white battlemented **Tower**, constructed between 1212 and 1305, and the **Temple of Minerva**, the great Roman monument of Assisi, both made famous by Giotto and the « Maestro della Santa Cecilia » in the painting in the Basilica (cf. page 16).

TEMPLE OF MINERVA (*Santa Maria Sopra Minerva, now St. Philip Neri*). - The Christian title given to this edifice is the same as that of the one existing in Rome and was given for similar reasons, with the difference that here in Assisi the pagan temple was not destroyed or built over with a Christian church when it was converted from pagan to Christian use, but only altered internally, with the perfect façade left exactly as it was. The temple was dedicated to the goddess Minerva and goes back to the beginning of the age of the Roman emperors, and is one of the best preserved of its kind. The harmonious frontage is composed of a **pronaos** or outer vestibule with six elegant fluted Corinthian columns and a pediment and tympanum, all of marble, to which time has given the beautiful patina of old ivory. One of the most interesting things about the temple is that for technical reasons the architect was unable to lay the usual spacious flight of steps in front, and so had the brilliant idea of creating an optical illusion by inserting the steps between the columns and thereby creating a pleasing and original design.

THE ROMAN FORUM (*Archeological Museum*). - It is one of the most impressive places in this extraordinary town that is so full of surprises. Actually it is the ground space of the ancient forum preserved a few yards below the level of the street which was raised in succeeding ages, and in parts it still retains the original paving. The dimly-lit underground passages have all the charm of buried things. The fragments of stone tablets along the sides record events in the life of the ancient Roman **Assisium** (some inscriptions belong to the **Gens Propertia,** the family from which the poet Propertius was descended), and one can see the foundations of the Temple of Minerva which also lie buried. The work of excavation and archeological research has been recently resumed and continues with notable results.

SAN RUFINO (*Cathedral*). - Its chief thing is the façade, covering the far end of a small square wich seems made to measure, and which you reach in the right frame of mind after a long climb up a street (**Via San Rufino**) that still remains completely mediaeval. This façade of Assisi Cathedral is one of the most splendid in Umbria, measured, logical and coherent, perfection itself. The tall massive Romanesque bell-tower stands proudly on one side. The reasoned geometrical scheme of the rectangular divisions, outlined by slender cornices in the lower part (the most ancient), solemnly dissolves and expands into the threefold central space after the golden interruption of the **loggetta** with its suspended arches. Above it the three magnificent rose-windows (the recurrent theme of Assisian architecture) usher in the completion of the façade in triangular form, flanking the superb upward soaring of the great Gothic arch. The architectural design is flawless, such as few others are to be found. The three doorways, preceded by lions and griffins, are adorned with designs of strange animals, and the lunettes with essential relief-work.

Dedicated to Rufino, saint and bishop and official protector of Assisi, the church was begun in the 9th century, enlarged in the 11th, completely remade by Giovanni da Gubbio under Bishop Ugone in 1144, and restored in 1217, the last consecration being in 1228.

SANTA CHIARA. - Its façade is a colourful and skilful alternation of the different hues of rose-white and violet-red of the marble of Subasio. The architectural composition resembles it in its simplicity - two superimposed horizontal zones with a tympanum, an arched doorway with an imitation vestibule, and the usual splendid rose window through which pours the magic light of the Umbrian sunset, reflecting the sea of green from the square in front (this square is Assisi's balcony from which you have a view of the whole of the plain beneath). The characteristic feature of the church is the flying buttesses that spring daringly upwards to support the sides. Those on the right are walled over, with the convent, cloister and nuns' garden behind them; the others on the left form a light-filled three-arched passageway. The church was founded in 1257 and consecrated in 1265.

This time the interior does not delude. Just as the exterior does, it derives inspiration from the Basilica of San Francesco, whose architectural and spatial form it reproduces in general terms (with side chapels added, naturally). In the way of painting as well, Santa Chiara is the church that has most to offer after the Basilica: the cycles of frescoes of the school of Giotto in the apse, the others in the transept arms (two of the 14th century), the Florentine and Sienese ones in the Blessed Sacrament chapel, and finally the oil paintings on wood, especially the dramatic 13th century **Crucifix** in the apse and the hieratic **St. Clare** in the transept, both by the 13th century « Maestro di Santa Chiara ».

While the body of the first great woman-Franciscan lies in pomp and splendour in a shrine under the vaults of the crypt, in the church a place of honour is reserved for the ancient Byzantine crucifix that spoke to St. Francis in San Damiano and was later brought here.

**THE CRUCIFIX
OF SAN DAMIANO**
(*Church of Santa Chiara*).

45

**ST. CLARE AND
EIGHT STORIES
OF HER LIFE**
(*Church
of Santa Chiara*).

SANTA MARIA MAGGIORE. - It stands in a tree-lined square which is suspended in mid-air between town and country and set there as if to provide a necessary pause in one of the most picturesque and inspiring walks through Assisi. The 12th century church is another triumph of Romanesque which as we have seen is native to Assisi, and the builder bears an illustrious name - the same Giovanni da Gubbio who remade the interior of the Cathedral and who is commemorated on a stone tablet on the façade, dated 1163. The façade is simple in style, and the fine bell-tower as well is built on the traditional lines of Assisi Romanesque. The interior is attractive with three naves divided by columns, and unusual for the different kinds of roofing (wooden beams in the middle nave, vaulting in the side ones). The foundations are Roman, as recent archeological findings have shown.

Alongside it in the square is the *Vescovado* (Bishop's Palace) which played an important role in the life of Francis. It was the scene of his sensational renunciation of worldly goods, and it was here he took shelter when he lay ill and suffering in 1226.

AN ITINERARY THROUGH ASSISI
(from Santa Chiara to San Pietro)

This is only one example chosen from among the numerous ones that this unique town is able to offer. In this case, too, you must know how to move backwards in time and let yourself be transported into the magic of the distant past. If you can make the effort the result will be rewarding, and you will find that the Middle Ages speak with a voice of extraordinary power and persuasiveness.

To begin with, the steep narrow street called Via Sant'Agnese is quite medieval. It makes its curving way down till we come to the picturesque remains of Roman walls, and then begins one of those charming features of the streets of Assisi which seem made on purpose but are actually quite accidental - the sudden spectacular openings on to the countryside which take you by surprise, revealing almost limitless vistas and obliging you to pause and gaze. You begin to climb after Santa Maria Maggiore and continue along streets quite as remarkable, **Via Cristofani** or **Via San Bernardo di Chiaravalle**, with ancients walls, small stone and brick houses and an overflowing of balconies. You have to resist the temptation to go up or down through other enticing streets and lanes like **Via San Gregorio**, **Via degli Ancaiani**, **Vicolo Frondini**, and so many others that are full of houses of saints and confraternities and of oratories. In Via Fontebella you can see the tall tower-houses (the oldest is that of the **Monte Frumentario**), at the foot of which you are welcomed by the refreshing coolness of the 16th century fountain, **Fonte Marcella**. From here a few yards brings you to **Porta San Francesco** and, as if by magic, on turning left down a hill incredibly crowded with antique and souvenir shops, both sacred and profane (**Piaggia di Porta San Pietro**), you find yourself in front of yet another gate of the town, that of St. Peter, and a square with a church of the same name which has remained intact, one of the most beautiful examples of Romano-Gothic architecture in Assisi.

A delightful view of the **Rocca Maggiore** and Piazza Santa Chiara seen through one of the flying buttresses on the church of Santa Chiara.

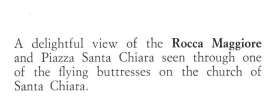

A picturesque corner of old Assisi: **Borgo San Pietro** with its characteristic wrought-iron work. ▶

CHURCH OF SAN PIETRO. - The façade of this Benedictine church is, like the others, logically and geometrically conceived, with polished surfaces between pilasters and small arches that seem made on purpose to allow a free play of the varied hues of stone and marble from Subasio. Once again there are the magnificent rose-windows, threefold and marble-ringed, here set in an ample and masterly way, and a main doorway adorned with precious friezework. It is easy to imagine what the façade was like before the destruction of its triangular top, similar to those on the façades of San Francesco and the Cathedral. The church dates from the 12th century and was rebuilt in the 13th, and the massive square-shaped bell-tower is also Romanesque.

The striking things inside are the expressive language of the bare walls and vaulting, the ruggedness of the few essential pillars. An awesome light, descending from above through the glass in the dome built of concentric rows of stone, creates the gloom of an Etruscan or Roman temple; the arches of the lateral naves are the traditional ones of Romanesque, fully rounded, while those of the cross-vault and central nave under the wooden roofing are pointed Gothic. The whole effect is stupendous, and architecturally perhaps the finest of any church in Assisi, showing the gradual transformation of Romanesque into Gothic.

SANTO STEFANO. - To reach this small 13th century church — one of the most Franciscan in its bare simplicity — you have to climb up stony lanes and flights of wide steps. Both outside and inside it is built only on essential lines, and in the single silent nave there are still traces of old frescoes. The most interesting thing about the church is undoubtedly the Romanesque apse. Viewed from outside, overtopped by the slender brick tower, it gives a pleasing pictorial effect in the skilful blending of the coloured marble of the tracery on the pilasters and especially on the elegantly-designed arches.

THE ROCCA MAGGIORE (Citadel).

- Assisi too has its fortress. Actually it has two, a smaller one as well, but this, the **Maggiore**, proudly sited astride the summit of the mountain spur, is much more important than the other **Minore**. It has an ancient history of long and troubled times which is reflected in the many changes it has undergone. At first it was a Swabian fortress, one of the many imperial strongholds scattered throughout Italy, and for a time was the dwelling of the young Frederick II when he was entrusted to the care of a guardian, Duke Conrad of Lutzen. In 1198 it was lost to the imperial forces and destroyed in a wave of popular fury. Rebuilt by Albornoz in 1367, it was enlarged by Pius II and Sixtus IV in the following century, and the circular rampart was added between 1535 and 1538 by Paul III, the same pope who built the « Rocca Paolina » at Perugia. It can thus serve as a text-book of the art of fortification from the Middle Ages to the Renaissance.

Unfortunately the towers, ramparts, fortified enclosures, communication trenches, corridors, guard posts etc. are now in a state of serious decay, the common destiny of castles almost everywhere today. Against this there is the view it offers, magnificent and almost boundless, over the town and the great plain on one side, and the shady winding valley of the Tescio on the other.

LOGGIA OF THE MONTE FRUMENTARIO - OLIVIE-RA FOUNTAIN.

The ancient **Monte Frumentario** eloquently faces Via San Francesco with a finely-built **loggia,** or portico, which is one of the most representative of Assisi, and one of the most interesting of its civic monuments. Dating from 1267, it is composed of a row of seven columns supporting lowered and edged arches, crowned on top by a series of small trilobe ones. Under the portico there are still preserved fragments of 14th century frescoes. Beside the portico and on a line with it is the beautiful **Fonte Oliviera**, one of the many fountains that used to be in Assisi, which takes its name from Messer Oliviero Lodovici who had it built *ad publicam utilitatem* — for public use — in 1570.

L'EREMO DELLE CARCERI (The Prison-Hermitage). -

The road is long and sunbeaten, without shade though lined on both sides by seedling nurseries. You leave Assisi by the Porta dei Cappuccini and as you proceed the town becomes smaller and smaller in the distance, but you never lose sight of it completely (it is there at every turn of the road as you climb up Subasio). Needless to say, the views from here round about Assisi are the same splendid ones as ever.

You suddenly find yourself in the cool freshness of a forest of green and you are already at the gate of the Hermitage, over 2,560 ft. high. This was the refuge place of Francis who, as the story says, « *loved to flee the companionship of men and retire into remote places... in the blessed solitude of contemplation* ». It is also said that it was here that he first received the call from God. You can still see the ancient oratory that the Benedictines gave to Francis and the grotto cut out of the rock with his stone bed. The monastery which was built later by San Bernardino in the 15th century preserves the memory of the early Franciscan ideal with the passages and cells cut out of the mountainside and the poor roughly-made furniture, and the pervading atmosphere of heavenly peace and calm. Outside in the virgin forest there are still the scattered and isolated « refuges » of Francis's humble and saintly companions, Bernardo, Silvestro, Rufino, Leone, Masseo. The friar who accompanies you will show you the age-old tree that tradition holds to be the scene of the preaching to the birds.

RIVOTORTO. - The place takes its name from the stream that flows by it through the plain. You reach it from Assisi through the San Francesco Gate after a couple of miles' walk. The church you see there has nothing extraordinary about it. It is imitation Gothic and was built in 1854 to replace the 16th century one destroyed in an earthquake, but inside it is preserved one of the most valuable records — and one of the earliest — of the Franciscan movement, the **Tugurio**, the low-roofed rustic hovel built of roughly hewn stones, where in the April of 1208 Francis and his first two followers, Pietro Cattani and Bernardo da Quintavalle, assembled for the first time. Rivotorto was therefore the first Franciscan convent, and the event is recorded by an inscription over the doorway of the church: HIC PRIMORDIA FRATUM MINORUM (Here was the beginning of the Friars Minor).

SAN DAMIANO

A long white road between fields, vineyards and olive groves. Assisi lies behind you while you have sight of Subasio immeasurably enlarged in the brownness of its woods, the old and newly planted ones, and the great plain of Umbria draws nearer. A road for pilgrims and begging friars. All that is sacred in the air of Assisi seems to become intensified here as if in proximity to a miracle. Another stretch of downward slope, steeper than before. A high wall on the other side of which the tops of tall cypresses are swaying gently. A small square paved with grey stones, the soft purring of a nearby invisible fountain, a roughly designed façade and a low, unsymmetrical portico leading into a church,

the round window at which Clare of Assisi stood holding a monstrance on a Friday in September 1241 and put to flight the Saracen hordes that Frederick II was preparing to hurl against Assisi. More than any other place, San Damiano is the focal point of the spiritual and poetic adventure of Francis and Clare. While yet a girl, Clare came here with a few companions and led here her saintly life till the day of her death on August 11th, 1253, in the great bare room on the first floor where the swallows still make their nests and fly away with a rustling noise at the sound of a visitor's footsteps. Her roof-garden is only a few square feet in measurement but is pregnant with the air of Umbria. « *When she returned*

from prayer, her face would seem brighter and lovelier than the sun. » The prayers of Clare and her sisters still seem to resound in the rough wooden stalls in the choir.

But before her, at the beginning of the century, Francis had already come to San Damiano, mysteriously drawn to pray in the tumbledown half-ruined oratory that it then was. Here in 1205 he heard the voice from the crucifix saying to him, « *Go, Francis, and repair my house* ». And Francis, obedient to the command of Christ, restored the church with his own hands and « *sweated with marvellous zeal* ». It was here, then, that the great and humble Franciscan epic began.

He came back to San Damiano again, and spent the winter of 1224-25 in a poor hut below Clare's garden, still bleeding from the wounds of the stigmata which he had just received. Here according to tradition he wrote the « *Canticle of Creatures* »:

« *Praise to thee, my Lord, with all thy creatures.* » The chapel repaired by Francis is a humble one, low-vaulted, of rough-hewn stones, blackened by the years and the smoke of incense and candles, but the feeling of spirituality in it is intense. A few ancient frescoes remain, like the one of uncertain authorship on the right wall relating « stories » of the saint, and another early 14th one in the apse with the Madonna, San Damiano and San Rufino. The Poor Clares used to receive Communion through a small window in the choir where the names of the first of the sisters remain, and where there is the niche in which Francis one day took refuge to escape from his irate father. All is holy and serene in the bare refectory, in St. Clare's small oratory (Frate Leone's breviary is preserved there among other things), in the dormitory and the infirmary. This must have been the birthplace of Franciscan « charitas ».

SANTA MARIA DEGLI ANGELI
(THE PORZIUNÇOLA)

vides a sharp contrast to the **Cappellina**, the tiny rustic church inside in the centre of the nave, with its air of pure spirituality, and no less to the moving, still smaller chapel of the **Transito** where Francis died lying on the bare ground, half hidden in the shadow of the huge wall. It is better to think of these surviving records of one of the greatest adventures of the spirit as they were originally, half concealed among trees, meadows and marshy land and open to the free flight of birds and angels.

Around the church and joined to it are the most sacred and famous places of Franciscan history and legend: the saint's cell in the **Cappella delle Rose,** and the still more famous **Roseta** or rose garden among whose thorns one tormented night Francis found shelter and relief from a harassing temptation. Around the saint's shrine his beloved turtle doves still make their nests (« *O sisters of mine, you simple doves, chaste and innocent, why do you let ourselves be caught? I want you to be saved from death and build your nests here, so that you may bear fruit and multiply according to your Creator's command* »).

Let us end by saying that here at the Porziuncola is the beginning and the end of all the roads that lead to Francis, the starting and finishing point of all the pilgrimages made in the footsteps of the great mystic and poet of Assisi.

◀ The chapel of the *Porziuncola*, where the first
followers of St. Francis gathered to meet, is
still preserved in the middle of the Basilica
of Santa Maria degli Angeli. A nineteenth-cen-
tury fresco by G. F. Overbeck is shown on
the front.

voices had been heard in it. In 1209, when the
rule of the order had been approved, Francis ob-
tained the use of the wood and the chapel from
the Benedictines, and the first poor huts of his
followers grew up round about, so that the Por-

ziuncola became the gathering place and a kind
of headquarters for the Franciscans. In 1215 the
first general chapter of the Order was held there,
and every year therefter (in 1221 there were already five thousand friars). Clare took her
vows there in March 1212, and Francis died there
on 3rd October 1226. Thus the Porziuncola is
intimately connected with a large part of the
« heroic » period of the Franciscan movement.
Though there is nothing that can be said against
the strictly logical conception of the design, the
magnificence and pomposity of Alessi's church,
typical of the Counter-Reformation period, pro-

In his well-known poem on Santa Maria degli Angeli Carducci made the mistake of attributing the dome of the church to Vignola instead of to Alessi, but the mistake was not so serious after all, as Vignola had something to do with it, even if it was only to give his authoritative opinion about it.

The dome, besides springing daringly upwards, seems to project its 'zone of influence' over a wide range all around, and is the actual centre of perspective for the whole of the plain of Assisi. The great basilica was built at the desire of Pius V who wished to give a fit and worthy habitation to what remained of Francis's **Porziuncola**, and at the same time provide a more ample place of gathering for the hundreds of pilgrims who flock here every year for the feast of the **Pardon** on the Ist and 2nd of August. Designed by Galeazzo Alessi, the church took over a century to build (1569-1679), but a large part of it was destroyed by earthquakes in 1832 leaving only the façade intact. It was rebuilt shortly afterwards by Poletti in identical form, but in 1928 the present great façade was laid over the 16th century one by Bazzani and was modelled chiefly on the Roman Baroque style.

The name **Porziuncola**, it should be remembered, originally referred only to a « small piece » of land (in mediaeval Latin *portiuncula*) belonging to the Benedictines of Subasio. It was wooded country in which there was a small chapel popularly called St. Mary of the Angels because angelic

INDEX